ROYAL COURT

Royal Court Theatre presents

MOUNTAIN LANGUAGE

First performed at the Royal National Theatre on 20 October 1988.

ASHES TO ASHES

First performed at the Royal Court on 12 September 1996.

by **Harold Pinter**

Performed at the Royal Court Jerwood Theatre Downstairs,
Sloane Square, London on 21 June 2001.

The Royal Court is presenting Ashes to Ashes and Mountain Language as part of the Lincoln Center
Festival's season of Harold Pinter's plays in New York, July 2001.

MOUNTAIN LANGUAGE

Cast in order of appearance
Elderly Woman **Gabrielle Hamilton**
Young Woman **Anastasia Hille**
Sergeant **Neil Dudgeon**
Officer **Geoffrey Streatfeild**
Prisoner **Paul Hilton**
Guard **Daniel Cerqueira**
Second Guard **Tim Treloar**

ASHES TO ASHES

Devlin **Neil Dudgeon**
Rebecca **Anastasia Hille**

by **Harold Pinter**

Director **Katie Mitchell**
Designer **Vicki Mortimer**
Lighting Designer **Paule Constable**
Sound Designer **Gareth Fry**
Assistant Director **Nina Raine**
Casting **Lisa Makin, Amy Ball**
Production Manager **Paul Handley**
Company Stage Manager **Cath Binks**
Stage Manager **Pea Horsley**
Deputy Stage Manager **Claire Lovett**
Assistant Stage Manager **Maxine Foo**
Costume Supervisor **Iona Kenrick**
Company Voice Work **Patsy Rodenburg**

Royal Court Theatre would like to thank the following for their help with this production:
Peter Jones, Wardrobe care by Persil and Comfort courtesy of Lever Brothers Ltd.

THE COMPANY

Harold Pinter (writer)
For the Royal Court: Ashes To Ashes, The New World Order.
Other theatre includes: The Room; The Birthday Party; A Slight Ache; The Hothouse; The Caretaker; A Night Out, Night School; The Dwarfs; The Collection; The Lover; Tea Party; The Homecoming; The Basement; Landscape; Silence; Old Times; Monologue; No Man's Land; Betrayal; Family Voices; A Kind of Alaska; Victoria Station; One for the Road; Mountain Language; Party Time; Moonlight; Celebration.
Film includes: The Caretaker, The Pumpkin Eater, The Servant, The Quiller Memorandum, Accident, The Birthday Party, The Go-Between, The Homecoming, Langrishe Go Down, A La Recherche Du Temps Perdu, The Last Tycoon, The French Lieutenant's Woman, Betrayal, Victory, Turtle Diary, The Handmaid's Tale, Reunion, The Heat of the Day, The Comfort of Strangers, The Trial.
Awards include: CBE, Shakespeare Prize (Hamburg), European Prize for Literature (Vienna), Pirandello Prize (Palermo), The David Cohen British Literature Prize, Laurence Olivier Special Award, a Moliere d'Honneur, The Golden Pen Award, The Critics' Circle Award for Distinguished Service to the Arts (2000), The Brianza Poetry Prize, Italy 2000 and the South Bank Award for Outstanding Achievement in the Arts, 2001. He has also received 14 Honorary Doctorates.

Daniel Cerqueira
For the Royal Court: Cleansed, Attempts on Her Life, The Crutch (Young Writers Festival 1999), Bintou, International New Playwrights 2000.
Other theatre includes: Two Tigers (Edinburgh Festival); Caledonian Road (White Bear); Blue Vienna (Hampstead); Ten Years of Freedom, Crocodile Looking at Birds (Lyric, Hammersmith); Courting Winona (Old Red Lion); Waking Beauty (Arts Threshold); Days of Hope (Oxford Stage Co.); The Brave (Bush); Handsome, Handicapped and Hebrew (Grove); Antony and Cleopatra (Moving Theatre Company); The Art of Random Whistling, The People Downstairs (Young Vic); Aunt Dan and Lemon (Almeida); Powder Keg (Gate); Meat (Plymouth Theatre Royal); Luminosity (RSC); While Waiting at My Mother's Vigil (BAC).
Television includes: Pirate Prince, Hot Dog Wars, City Central, Sunburn.
Film includes: Valley Girls, Saving Private Ryan, Toy Boys, Mad Cows, Tube Tales.

Paule Constable (lighting designer)
For the Royal Court: Presence, Credible Witness, The Country, Dublin Carol, The Weir, The Glory of Living.
Other theatre includes: The Seagull, Tales from Ovid, The Dispute, Uncle Vanya, Beckett Shorts, The Mysteries (RSC); The Villains' Opera, Darker Face of the Earth, Haroun and the Sea of Stories, Caucasian Chalk Circle (RNT); Amadeus (West End, Broadway, Olivier nomination); Les Miserables (Tel Aviv); The Servant (Lyric); More Grimms' Tales (Young Vic and New York); four productions for Theatre de Complicite including the Olivier-nominated Street of Crocodiles.
Opera includes: productions for the English National Opera, Welsh National Opera, Scottish Opera, Opera North, Glyndebourne, La Monnaie.

Neil Dudgeon
For the Royal Court: Blasted, Road, Waiting Room Germany, Talking in Tongues, No One Sees the Video, Shirley.
Other theatre includes: Closer, Yerma, School For Wives (RNT); The Importance of Being Earnest, Richard II (Royal Exchange Manchester); Crackwalker (Gate); Miss Julie (Oldham Coliseum); The Next Best Thing (Nuffield); The Daughter-in-Law (Bristol Old Vic); A Collier's Friday Night (Greenwich); The Changeling (Cambridge Theatre Co & tour); School For Scandal (Cambridge Theatre).
Television includes: Messiah, Dirty Tricks, Mrs Bradley Mysteries, Four Fathers, Tom Jones, The Gift, Our Boy, Breakout, Out of the Blue, The All New Alexi Sayle Show, Common As Muck, Fatherland, Touch of Frost, Sharpes Eagles, Between the Lines, Resnick, Nightvoice, Saracen, Piece of Cake, Road.
Film includes: It was an Accident, Revolver, Breathtaking, Crossing the Border, Fools of Fortune, Red King, White Knight, Prick Up Your Ears.
Awards include: Best Actor for Single Film at the Monte Carlo Television Awards for The Gift.

Gareth Fry (sound designer)
For the Royal Court: The Country.
Other theatre includes: The Oresteia (RNT);
Noise of Time, Mnemonic, The Street of
Crocodiles (Theatre de Complicite); Wexford
Trilogy (Oxford Stage Company); Play to Win
(Soho Theatre & national tour).

Gabrielle Hamilton
For the Royal Court: Across the Divide, King
Kong's Daughter.
Other theatre includes: Crown Matrimonial
(Sheringham Norfolk); You be Ted and I'll be
Sylvia (Hampstead); Pygmalion (Vienna,
European tour); The Importance of Being
Earnest (UK tour); Listen to the Wind (Kings
Head); Tartuffe (Almeida); Forty Years On
(Dukes, Lancaster); Unlawful Killing, Great
Expectations, Salonica (Wolsey, Ipswich);
My Mother Said I Never Should (Palace
Westcliffe); Ten Times Table (Salisbury
Playhouse); Tovarich (Piccadilly); Arsenic and
Old Lace, Henry VII, Tovarich (Chichester
Festival); Sauce for the Goose (Nuffield
Southampton); A Doll's House (Haymarket
Leicester); Under the Web (Soho Poly);
Hobson's Choice (Leeds Playhouse); Just
Between Ourselves (Everyman Cheltenham);
Martine (Leatherhead); Bed Before Yesterday,
The Unvarnished Truth (Phoenix Theatre, Derek
Nimmo Company); Separate Tables (Exeter,
Northcott).
Television includes: My Hero, Active Defence,
Casualty, Tube Tales, Silent Witness, Rough
Justice, Crime Monthly, Fist of Fun, Surgical
Spirit, Knowing You Knowing Me, The Great
Kadinsky, Mayhew's London, Frank Stubbs,
Inspector Wycliffe, Eastenders, Tomorrow
People, An Unwanted Woman, I.T., Never the
Twain, Bookmark - Adam, The Chief, Strike it
Rich, Secret Garden, Tales of the Unexpected,
Shroud For a Nightingale.

Anastasia Hille
Theatre includes: Therese Raquin, Uncle Vanya,
The Maids (Young Vic); Arms and the Man
(Cambridge Theatre Company); The Oresteia,
Richard III, Macbeth (RNT); Measure for
Measure, The Duchess of Malfi (Cheek By Jowl);
Three Tall Women (Wyndhams); The Two
Gentlemen of Verona, A Mad World My Masters,
As You Like It (Globe); Morphic Resonance
(Donmar Warehouse).
Television includes: Kavanagh QC, Eleven Men
Against Eleven, Trial & Retribution, Dance to the
Music of Time, Big Women, Storm Damage,
RKO 281, The Cazalet Chronicle.
Film includes: Wisdom of Crocodiles, Escort,
New Year's Day, Five Seconds to Spare.
Radio includes: Desdemona and Othello.

Paul Hilton
Theatre includes: Les Blancs, Ghosts
(Manchester Royal Exchange); The Oresteia
(RNT); Three Sisters (Oxford Stage Company);
The Storm (Almeida); As You Like It, A Mad
World My Masters (Shakespeare's Globe);
Woyzcek, Endgame, The Mysteries, Romeo and
Juliet, The Cherry Orchard, Richard III (RSC);
Twelfth Night, A Small Family Business, Stone
Free (Bristol Old Vic).
Radio includes: The White Guard, As You Like
It, Robin Hood's Revenge, Mysteries.
Paul was nominated for the Ian Charleson
Award 1998/99.

Katie Mitchell (director)
For the Royal Court: The Country.
Other theatre includes: A Woman Killed With
Kindness, The Dybbuk, Ghosts, Henry VI,
Easter, Phoenician Woman, The Mysteries,
Beckett Shorts, Uncle Vanya (with The Young
Vic) (RSC); Rutherford and Son, The Machine
Wreckers, The Oresteia (RNT); Iphigenia at
Aulis, The Last Ones (Abbey Dublin); Endgame
(Donmar Warehouse); Attempts On Her Life
(Piccolo Teatro di Milano); The Maids (Young
Vic).
Opera includes: Don Giovanni, Jenufa and Katya
Kabanova (Welsh National Opera).
Awards include: 1996 Evening Standard Award
for Best Director for The Phoenician Woman
(RSC).

Vicki Mortimer (designer)
For the Royal Court: The Country, My Zinc
Bed.
Other theatre includes: The Maids (Young Vic);
The Real Thing (Donmar); The Seagull, A
Woman Killed with Kindness, The Dybbuk,
Ghosts, Phoenician Women, Beckett Shorts,
Uncle Vanya, The Creation, The Passion (RSC);
The Oresteia, Rutherford & Son, The Machine
Wreckers, Fair Ladies at a Game of Poem
Cards, Closer (RNT); 1953, Heartbreak House
(Almeida); Therese Raquin, 'Tis Pity She's a
Whore, Hedda Gabler, L'Aigle a Deux Tetes,
The Changeling, Three Sisters, Lady Aoi, Hanjo,
Electra, Lulu, The Triumph of Love (Theatre
Project Tokyo).
Opera includes: Salome (ENO); Jenufa, Katya
Kabanova (Welsh National Opera); The Turn of
the Screw (Scottish Opera).
Dance includes: Millenium, Sulpher 16, Aeon
(Random Dance Co.).

Nina Raine (assistant director)
For the Royal Court: Presence, Mouth To
Mouth, Far Away, My Zinc Bed.
Theatre includes: Passion Play, Miss Julie (Burton
Taylor Theatre, Oxford); The Way of the World
(for the Red Cross at Trebinshwyn); Ashes to
Ashes.
Nina is currently on the Regional Theatre Young
Director Scheme at the Royal Court Theatre.

Geoffrey Streatfeild
Theatre includes: Henry VI Parts 1, 2 & 3,
Richard III (RSC).
Television includes: Love in a Cold Climate,
Sword of Honour.
Awards include: Behrens Bursary, Laurence
Olivier Award 1999 in association with the
Society of London Theatre.

Tim Treloar
Theatre includes: Richard II, Romeo & Juliet,
Back To Methuselah (RSC); Hamlet, Heartpiece
(RSC Fringe); The Night Before Christmas (RSC,
Bridewell).
Television includes: Bomber.
Film includes: Morning Was Broken.
Radio includes: Pierre Jean, The Weekend Starts
Here, Richard II, As You Like It.
Awards include: BBC Carleton Hobbs Award
1999.

THE ENGLISH STAGE COMPANY AT THE ROYAL COURT

The English Stage Company at the Royal Court opened in 1956 as a subsidised theatre producing new British plays, international plays and some classical revivals.

The first artistic director George Devine aimed to create a writers' theatre, 'a place where the dramatist is acknowledged as the fundamental creative force in the theatre and where the play is more important than the actors, the director, the designer'. The urgent need was to find a contemporary style in which the play, the acting, direction and design are all combined. He believed that 'the battle will be a long one to continue to create the right conditions for writers to work in'.

Devine aimed to discover 'hard-hitting, uncompromising writers whose plays are stimulating, provocative and exciting'. The Royal Court production of John Osborne's Look Back in Anger in May 1956 is now seen as the decisive starting point of modern British drama and the policy created a new generation of British playwrights. The first wave included John Osborne, Arnold Wesker, John Arden, Ann Jellicoe, N F Simpson and Edward Bond. Early seasons included new international plays by Bertolt Brecht, Eugène Ionesco, Samuel Beckett, Jean-Paul Sartre and Marguerite Duras.

The theatre started with the 400-seat proscenium arch Theatre Downstairs, and then in 1969 opened a second theatre, the 60-seat studio Theatre Upstairs. Some productions transfer to the West End, such as Caryl Churchill's Far Away, Conor McPherson's The Weir, Kevin Elyot's Mouth to Mouth and My Night With Reg. The Royal Court also co-produces plays which have transferred to the West End or toured internationally, such as Sebastian Barry's The Steward of Christendom and Mark Ravenhill's Shopping and Fucking (with Out of Joint), Martin McDonagh's The Beauty Queen Of Leenane (with Druid Theatre Company), Ayub Khan-Din's East is East (with Tamasha Theatre Company, and now a feature film).

Since 1994 the Royal Court's artistic policy has again been vigorously directed to finding and producing a new generation of playwrights. The writers include Joe Penhall, Rebecca Prichard, Michael Wynne, Nick Grosso, Judy Upton, Meredith Oakes, Sarah Kane, Anthony Neilson, Judith Johnson, James Stock, Jez Butterworth, Marina Carr, Simon Block, Martin McDonagh, Mark Ravenhill, Ayub Khan-Din, Tamantha Hammerschlag, Jess Walters, Che Walker, Conor McPherson, Simon Stephens, Richard Bean, Roy

photo: Andy Chopping

Williams, Gary Mitchell, Mick Mahoney, Rebecca Gilman, Christopher Shinn, Kia Corthron, David Gieselmann, Marius von Mayenburg and David Eldridge. This expanded programme of new plays has been made possible through the support of A.S.K Theater Projects, the Jerwood Charitable Foundation, the American Friends of the Royal Court Theatre and many in association with the Royal National Theatre Studio.

In recent years there have been record-breaking productions at the box office, with capacity houses for Jez Butterworth's Mojo, Sebastian Barry's The Steward of Christendom, Martin McDonagh's The Beauty Queen of Leenane, Ayub Khan-Din's East is East, Eugène Ionesco's The Chairs, David Hare's My Zinc Bed and Conor McPherson's The Weir, which transferred to the West End in October 1998 and ran for nearly two years at the Duke of York's Theatre.

The newly refurbished theatre in Sloane Square opened in February 2000, with a policy still inspired by the first artistic director George Devine. The Royal Court is an international theatre for new plays and new playwrights, and the work shapes contemporary drama in Britain and overseas.

REBUILDING THE ROYAL COURT

In 1995, the Royal Court was awarded a National Lottery grant through the Arts Council of England, to pay for three quarters of a £26m project to completely rebuild our 100-year old home. The rules of the award required the Royal Court to raise £7.6m in partnership funding. The building has been completed thanks to the generous support of those listed below.

We are particularly grateful for the contributions of over 5,700 audience members.

Royal Court Registered Charity number 231242.

THE AMERICAN FRIENDS OF THE ROYAL COURT THEATRE

AFRCT support the mission of the Royal Court and are primarily focused on raising funds to enable the theatre to produce new work by emerging American writers. Since this not-for-profit organisation was founded in 1997, AFRCT has contributed to seven productions including Rebecca Gilman's Spinning Into Butter. They have also supported the participation of young artists in the Royal Court's acclaimed International Residency.

If you would like to support the ongoing work of the Royal Court, please contact the Development Department on 020 7565 5050.

THE ARTS COUNCIL OF ENGLAND

PROGRAMME SUPPORTERS

The Royal Court (English Stage Company Ltd) receives its principal funding from London Arts. It is also supported financially by a wide range of private companies and public bodies and earns the remainder of its income from the box office and its own trading activities.

The Royal Borough of Kensington & Chelsea gives an annual grant to the Royal Court Young Writers' Programme and the London Boroughs Grants Committee provides project funding for a number of play development initiatives.

The Jerwood Charitable Foundation continues to support new plays by new playwrights through the Jerwood New Playwrights series. Since 1993 the A.S.K. Theater Projects of Los Angeles has funded a Playwrights' Programme at the theatre. Bloomberg Mondays, the Royal Court's reduced price ticket scheme, is supported by Bloomberg.

Sky has also generously committed to a two-year sponsorship of the Royal Court Young Writers' Festival.

TRUSTS AND FOUNDATIONS
American Friends of the Royal Court Theatre
The Carnegie United Kingdom Trust
Carlton Television Trust
Gerald Chapman Fund
Cultural Foundation Deutsche Bank
The Foundation for Sport and The Arts
The Genesis Foundation
The Goldsmiths Company
Jerwood Charitable Foundation
The John Lyons Charity
Laura Pels Foundation
Quercus Charitable Trust
The Peggy Ramsay Foundation
The Peter Sharp Foundation
The Royal Victoria Hall Foundation
The Sobell Foundation
The Trusthouse Charitable Foundation
Garfield Weston Foundation

MAJOR SPONSORS
A.S.K. Theater Projects
AT&T
Barclays plc
Bloomberg
Credit Suisse First Boston
Francis Finlay
Lever Fabergé (through Arts & Business New Partners)
Royal College of Psychiatrists
Sky

BUSINESS MEMBERS
BP
J Walter Thompson
Laporte plc
Lazard
Lever Fabergé
McCABES
Pemberton Greenish
Peter Jones
Redwood Publishing
Simons Muirhead & Burton

INDIVIDUAL MEMBERS
Patrons
Anon
David H Adams

Advanpress
Katie Bradford
Mrs Alan Campbell-Johnson
Gill Carrick
David Coppard
Chris Corbin
David Day
Thomas Fenton
Ralph A Fields
John Flower
Mike Frain
Edna & Peter Goldstein
David R & Catherine Graham
Phil Hobbs
Homevale Ltd
Mr & Mrs Jack Keenan
JHJ & SF Lewis
Lex Service plc
Barbara Minto
Michael & Mimi Naughton
New Penny Productions Ltd
Martin Newson
AT Poeton & Son Ltd.
André Ptaszynski, Really
Useful Theatres
Carolin Quentin
David Rowland
Sir George Russell
Ian Sellars
Bernard Shapero
Miriam Stoppard
Carl & Martha Tack
Jan & Michael Topham
Mr & Mrs Anthony Weldon
Richard Wilson OBE

Benefactors
Anon
Anastasia Alexander
Lesley E Alexander
Judith Asalache
Batia Asher
Elaine Mitchell Attias
Thomas Bendhem
Mark Bentley
Jody Berger
Keith & Helen Bolderson
Jeremy Bond
Brian Boylan
Mr & Mrs F H Bradley III
Mrs Elly Brook JP
Julian Brookstone
Paul & Ossi Burger
Debbi & Richard Burston
Yuen-Wei Chew
Martin Cliff

Carole & Neville Conrad
Conway Van Gelder
Coppard & Co.
Barry Cox
Curtis Brown Ltd
Deborah Davis
Zöe Dominic
Robyn Durie
Lorraine Esdaile
Winston & Jean Fletcher
Claire & William Frankel
Nick Fraser
Robert Freeman
J Garcia
Beverley & Nathaniel Gee
Norman Gerard
Henny Gestetner OBE
Jacqueline & Jonathan Gestetner
Michael Goddard
Carolyn Goldbart
Judy & Frank Grace
Sally Greene
Byron Grote
Sue & Don Guiney
Hamilton Asper Management
Woodley Hapgood
Jan Harris
Anna Home OBE
Amanda Howard Associates
Trevor Ingman
Lisa Irwin-Burgess
Peter Jones
Paul Kaju & Jane Peterson
Peter & Maria Kellner
Diana King
Clico Kingsbury
Lee & Thompson
Caroline & Robert Lee
C A Leng
Lady Lever
Colette & Peter Levy
Ann Lewis
Ian Mankin
Christopher Marcus
David Marks
Nicola McFarland
James McIvor
Mr & Mrs Roderick R McManigal
Mae Modiano
Eva Monley
Pat Morton
Georgia Oetker
Paul Oppenheimer

Janet & Michael Orr
Maria Peacock
Pauline Pinder
JTG Philipson QC
Jeremy Priestley
John & Rosemarie Reynolds
John Ritchie
Samuel French Ltd
Bernice & Victor Sandelson
John Sandoe (Books) Ltd
Nicholas Selmes
Lois Sieff OBE
Peregrine Simon
David & Patricia Smalley
Brian D Smith
John Soderquist
Max Stafford-Clark
Sue Stapely
Ann Marie Starr
June Summerill
Anthony Wigram
George & Moira Yip
Georgia Zaris

STAGE HANDS CIRCLE
Graham Billing
Andrew Cryer
Lindy Fletcher
Susan Hayden
Mr R Hopkins
Philip Hughes Trust
Dr A V Jones
Roger Jospe
Miss A Lind-Smith
Mr J Mills
Nevin Charitable Trust
Janet & Michael Orr
Jeremy Priestley
Ann Scurfield
Brian Smith
Harry Streets
Richard Wilson OBE
C C Wright

AWARDS FOR THE ROYAL COURT

Terry Johnson's Hysteria won the 1994 Olivier Award for Best Comedy, and also the Writers' Guild Award for Best West End Play. Kevin Elyot's My Night with Reg won the 1994 Writers' Guild Award for Best Fringe Play, the Evening Standard Award for Best Comedy, and the 1994 Olivier Award for Best Comedy. Joe Penhall was joint winner of the 1994 John Whiting Award for Some Voices. Sebastian Barry won the 1995 Writers' Guild Award for Best Fringe Play, the 1995 Critics' Circle Award and the 1997 Christopher Ewart-Biggs Literary Prize for The Steward of Christendom, and the 1995 Lloyds Private Banking Playwright of the Year Award. Jez Butterworth won the 1995 George Devine Award for Most Promising Playwright, the 1995 Writers' Guild New Writer of the Year Award, the Evening Standard Award for Most Promising Playwright and the 1995 Olivier Award for Best Comedy for Mojo.

The Royal Court won the 1995 Prudential Award for Theatre and was the overall winner of the 1995 Prudential Award for the Arts for creativity, excellence, innovation and accessibility. The Royal Court Theatre Upstairs won the 1995 Peter Brook Empty Space Award for innovation and excellence in theatre.

Michael Wynne won the 1996 Meyer-Whitworth Award for The Knocky. Martin McDonagh won the 1996 George Devine Award, the 1996 Writers' Guild Best Fringe Play Award, the 1996 Critics' Circle Award and the 1996 Evening Standard Award for Most Promising Playwright for The Beauty Queen of Leenane. Marina Carr won the 19th Susan Smith Blackburn Prize (1996/7) for Portia Coughlan. Conor McPherson won the 1997 George Devine Award, the 1997 Critics' Circle Award and the 1997 Evening Standard Award for Most Promising Playwright for The Weir. Ayub Khan-Din won the 1997 Writers' Guild Award for Best West End Play, the 1997 Writers' Guild New Writer of the Year Award and the 1996 John Whiting Award for East is East. Anthony Neilson won the 1997 Writers' Guild Award for Best Fringe Play for The Censor.

At the 1998 Tony Awards, Martin McDonagh's The Beauty Queen of Leenane (co-production with Druid Theatre Company) won four awards including Garry Hynes for Best Director and was nominated for a further two. Eugene Ionesco's The Chairs (co-production with Theatre de Complicite) was nominated for six Tony awards. David Hare won the 1998 Time Out Live Award for Outstanding Achievement and six awards in New York including the Drama League, Drama Desk and New York Critics Circle Award for Via Dolorosa. Sarah Kane won the 1998 Arts Foundation Fellowship in Playwriting. Rebecca Prichard won the 1998 Critics' Circle Award for Most Promising Playwright for Yard Gal (co-production with Clean Break).

Conor McPherson won the 1999 Olivier Award for Best New Play for The Weir. The Royal Court won the 1999 ITI Award for Excellence in International Theatre. Sarah Kane's Cleansed was judged Best Foreign Language Play in 1999 by Theater Heute in Germany. Gary Mitchell won the 1999 Pearson Best Play Award for Trust. Rebecca Gilman was joint winner of the 1999 George Devine Award and won the 1999 Evening Standard Award for Most Promising Playwright for The Glory of Living.

Roy Williams and Gary Mitchell were joint winners of the George Devine Award 2000 for Most Promising Playwright for Lift Off and The Force of Change respectively. At the Barclays Theatre Awards 2000 presented by the TMA, Richard Wilson won the Best Director Award for David Gieselmann's Mr Kolpert and Jeremy Herbert won the Best Designer Award for Sarah Kane's 4.48 Psychosis. Gary Mitchell won the Evening Standard's Charles Wintour Award 2000 for Most Promising Playwright for The Force of Change. Stephen Jeffreys' I Just Stopped by to See The Man won an AT&T: On Stage Award 2000. David Eldridge's Under the Blue Sky won the Time Out Live Award 2001 for Best New Play in the West End.

In 1999, the Royal Court won the European theatre prize New Theatrical Realities, presented at Taormina Arte in Sicily, for its efforts in recent years in discovering and producing the work of young British dramatists.

ROYAL COURT BOOKSHOP

The bookshop offers a wide range of playtexts, theatre books, screenplays and art-house videos with over 1,000 titles. Located in the downstairs Bar and Food area, the bookshop is open Monday to Saturday, afternoons and evenings.

Many Royal Court playtexts are available for just £2 including the plays in the current season and recent works by David Hare, Conor McPherson, Martin Crimp, Sarah Kane, David Mamet, Gary Mitchell, Martin McDonagh, Ayub Khan-Din, Jim Cartwright and Rebecca Prichard. We offer a 10% reduction to students on a range of titles.
Further information : 020 7565 5024

FOR THE ROYAL COURT

HAROLD PINTER

Mountain Language
&
Ashes to Ashes

ff

faber and faber

This collection first published in 2001
by Faber and Faber Limited
3 Queen Square, London WC1N 3AU

Typeset by Country Setting, Kingsdown, Kent CT14 8ES
Printed in England by Mackays of Chatham plc, Chatham, Kent

A CIP record for this book
is available from the British Library

0–571–21237–9

2 4 6 8 10 9 7 5 3 1

Contents

MOUNTAIN LANGUAGE

CHARACTERS

YOUNG WOMAN
ELDERLY WOMAN
SERGEANT
OFFICER
GUARD
PRISONER
HOODED MAN
SECOND GUARD

Mountain Language was first performed at the National Theatre, London, on 20 October 1988. The cast was as follows:

YOUNG WOMAN	Miranda Richardson
ELDERLY WOMAN	Eileen Atkins
SERGEANT	Michael Gambon
OFFICER	Julian Wadham
GUARD	George Harris
PRISONER	Tony Haygarth
HOODED MAN	Alex Hardy
SECOND GUARD	Douglas McFerran

Directed by Harold Pinter
Designed by Michael Taylor

One

A PRISON WALL

A line of women. An ELDERLY WOMAN, *cradling her hand. A basket at her feet. A* YOUNG WOMAN *with her arm around the* WOMAN's *shoulders.*

A SERGEANT *enters, followed by an* OFFICER. *The* SERGEANT *points to the* YOUNG WOMAN.

SERGEANT

Name!

YOUNG WOMAN

We've given our names.

SERGEANT

Name?

YOUNG WOMAN

We've given our names.

SERGEANT

Name?

OFFICER

(*To* SERGEANT) Stop this shit. (*To* YOUNG WOMAN) Any complaints?

YOUNG WOMAN

She's been bitten.

OFFICER

Who?

Pause.

Who? Who's been bitten?

YOUNG WOMAN

She has. She has a torn hand. Look. Her hand has been bitten. This is blood.

SERGEANT

(*To* YOUNG WOMAN) What is your name?

OFFICER

Shut up.

He walks over to ELDERLY WOMAN.

What's happened to your hand? Has someone bitten your hand?

The WOMAN *slowly lifts her hand. He peers at it.*

Who did this? Who bit you?

YOUNG WOMAN

A Dobermann pinscher.

6

OFFICER

Which one?

Pause.

Which one?

Pause.

Sergeant!

SERGEANT *steps forward.*

SERGEANT

Sir!

OFFICER

Look at this woman's hand. I think the thumb is going to come off. (*To* ELDERLY WOMAN) Who did this?

She stares at him.

Who did this?

YOUNG WOMAN

A big dog.

OFFICER

What was his name?

Pause.

What was his *name*?

Pause.

Every dog has a *name*! They answer to their name.
They are given a name by their parents and that is
their name, that is their *name*! Before they bite, they
state their name. It's a formal procedure. They state
their name and then they bite. What was his name?
If you tell me one of our dogs bit this woman without
giving his name I will have that dog shot!

Silence.

Now – attention! Silence and attention! Sergeant!

SERGEANT
Sir?

OFFICER
Take any complaints.

SERGEANT
Any complaints? Has anyone got any complaints?

YOUNG WOMAN
We were told to be here at nine o'clock this morning.

SERGEANT
Right. Quite right. Nine o'clock this morning.
Absolutely right. What's your complaint?

YOUNG WOMAN
We were here at nine o'clock this morning. It's now
five o'clock. We have been standing here for eight
hours. In the snow. Your men let Dobermann
pinschers frighten us. One bit this woman's hand.

OFFICER
What was the name of this dog?

She looks at him.

YOUNG WOMAN
I don't know his name.

SERGEANT
With permission sir?

OFFICER
Go ahead.

SERGEANT
Your husbands, your sons, your fathers, these men
you have been waiting to see, are shithouses. They are
enemies of the State. They are shithouses.

The OFFICER *steps towards the* WOMEN.

OFFICER

Now hear this. You are mountain people. You hear me? Your language is dead. It is forbidden. It is not permitted to speak your mountain language in this place. You cannot speak your language to your men. It is not permitted. Do you understand? You may not speak it. It is outlawed. You may only speak the language of the capital. That is the only language permitted in this place. You will be badly punished if you attempt to speak your mountain language in this place. This is a military decree. It is the law. Your language is forbidden. It is dead. No one is allowed to speak your language. Your language no longer exists. Any questions?

YOUNG WOMAN

I do not speak the mountain language.

Silence. The OFFICER *and* SERGEANT *slowly circle her. The* SERGEANT *puts his hand on her bottom.*

SERGEANT

What language do you speak? What language do you speak with your arse?

OFFICER

These women, Sergeant, have as yet committed no crime. Remember that.

SERGEANT

Sir! But you're not saying they're without sin?

OFFICER

Oh, no. Oh, no, I'm not saying that.

SERGEANT

This one's full of it. She bounces with it.

OFFICER

She doesn't speak the mountain language.

The WOMAN *moves away from the* SERGEANT'*s hand and turns to face the two men.*

YOUNG WOMAN

My name is Sara Johnson. I have come to see my husband. It is my right. Where is he?

OFFICER

Show me your papers.

She gives him a piece of paper. He examines it, turns to SERGEANT.

He doesn't come from the mountains. He's in the wrong batch.

SERGEANT

So is she. She looks like a fucking intellectual to me.

OFFICER

But you said her arse wobbled.

SERGEANT

Intellectual arses wobble the best.

Blackout.

Two

VISITORS ROOM

A PRISONER *sitting. The* ELDERLY WOMAN *sitting, with basket. A* GUARD *standing behind her.*

The PRISONER *and the* WOMAN *speak in a strong rural accent.*

Silence.

ELDERLY WOMAN

I have bread –

The GUARD *jabs her with a stick.*

GUARD

Forbidden. Language forbidden.

She looks at him. He jabs her.

It's forbidden. (*To* PRISONER) Tell her to speak the language of the capital.

PRISONER

She can't speak it.

Silence.

She doesn't speak it.

Silence.

ELDERLY WOMAN
I have apples –

The GUARD *jabs her and shouts.*

GUARD
Forbidden! Forbidden forbidden forbidden! Jesus
Christ! (*To* PRISONER) Does she understand what I'm
saying?

PRISONER
No.

GUARD
Doesn't she?

He bends over her.

Don't you?

She stares up at him.

PRISONER
She's old. She doesn't understand.

GUARD

Whose fault is that?

He laughs.

Not mine, I can tell you. And I'll tell you another thing. I've got a wife and three kids. And you're all a pile of shit.

Silence.

PRISONER

I've got a wife and three kids.

GUARD

You've what?

Silence.

You've got what?

Silence.

What did you say to me? You've got what?

Silence.

You've got *what*?

He picks up the telephone and dials one digit.

Sergeant? I'm in the Blue Room . . . yes . . . I thought I should report, Sergeant . . . I think I've got a joker in here.

Lights to half. The figures are still.

Voices over:

ELDERLY WOMAN'S VOICE
The baby is waiting for you.

PRISONER'S VOICE
Your hand has been bitten.

ELDERLY WOMAN'S VOICE
They are all waiting for you.

PRISONER'S VOICE
They have bitten my mother's hand.

ELDERLY WOMAN'S VOICE
When you come home there will be such a welcome for you. Everyone is waiting for you. They're all waiting for you. They're all waiting to see you.

Lights up. The SERGEANT *comes in.*

SERGEANT
What joker?

Blackout.

Three

VOICE IN THE DARKNESS

SERGEANT'S VOICE
Who's that fucking woman? What's that fucking
woman doing here? Who let that fucking woman
through that fucking door?

SECOND GUARD'S VOICE
She's his wife.

Lights up.

A corridor.

A HOODED MAN *held up by the* GUARD *and the*
SERGEANT. *The* YOUNG WOMAN *at a distance from
them, staring at them.*

SERGEANT
What is this, a reception for Lady Duck Muck?
Where's the bloody Babycham? Who's got the bloody
Babycham for Lady Duck Muck?

He goes to the YOUNG WOMAN.

Hello, Miss. Sorry. A bit of a breakdown in
administration, I'm afraid. They've sent you through

the wrong door. Unbelievable. Someone'll be done for this. Anyway, in the meantime, what can I do for you, dear lady, as they used to say in the movies?

Lights to half. The figures are still.

Voices over:

MAN'S VOICE
I watch you sleep. And then your eyes open. You look up at me above you and smile.

YOUNG WOMAN'S VOICE
You smile. When my eyes open I see you above me and smile.

MAN'S VOICE
We are out on a lake.

YOUNG WOMAN'S VOICE
It is spring.

MAN'S VOICE
I hold you. I warm you.

YOUNG WOMAN'S VOICE
When my eyes open I see you above me and smile.

Lights up. The HOODED MAN *collapses. The* YOUNG WOMAN *screams.*

YOUNG WOMAN

Charley!

The SERGEANT *clicks his fingers. The* GUARD *drags the* MAN *off.*

SERGEANT

Yes, you've come in the wrong door. It must be the computer. The computer's got a double hernia. But I'll tell you what – if you want any information on any aspect of life in this place we've got a bloke comes into the office every Tuesday week, except when it rains. He's right on top of his chosen subject. Give him a tinkle one of these days and he'll see you all right. His name is Dokes. Joseph Dokes.

YOUNG WOMAN

Can I fuck him? If I fuck him, will everything be all right?

Sure. No problem.

YOUNG WOMAN

Thank you.

Blackout.

Four

VISITORS ROOM

GUARD, ELDERLY WOMAN, PRISONER.

Silence.

The PRISONER *has blood on his face. He sits trembling. The* WOMAN *is still. The* GUARD *is looking out of a window. He turns to look at them both.*

GUARD
Oh, I forgot to tell you. They've changed the rules. She can speak. She can speak in her own language. Until further notice.

PRISONER
She can speak?

GUARD
Yes. Until further notice. New rules.

Pause.

PRISONER
Mother, you can speak.

Pause.

Mother, I'm speaking to you. You see? We can speak. You can speak to me in our own language.

She is still.

You can speak.

Pause.

Mother. Can you hear me? I am speaking to you in our own language.

Pause.

Do you hear me?

Pause.

It's our language.

Pause.

Can't you hear me? Do you hear me?

She does not respond.

Mother?

GUARD

Tell her she can speak in her own language. New rules. Until further notice.

PRISONER
Mother?

She does not respond. She sits still.

The PRISONER's *trembling grows. He falls from the chair on to his knees, begins to gasp and shake violently.*

The SERGEANT *walks into the room and studies the* PRISONER *shaking on the floor.*

SERGEANT
(*To* GUARD) Look at this. You go out of your way to give them a helping hand and they fuck it up.

Blackout.

ASHES TO ASHES

CHARACTERS

DEVLIN
REBECCA

Both in their forties

Time: Now

Ashes to Ashes was first presented by the Royal Court at the Ambassadors Theatre, London, on 12 September 1996. The cast was as follows:

DEVLIN   Stephen Rea
REBECCA   Lindsay Duncan

Directed by Harold Pinter
Designed by Eileen Diss
Lighting by Mick Hughes
Costume by Tom Rand
Sound by Tom Lishman

A house in the country.

Ground-floor room. A large window.
Garden beyond.

Two armchairs. Two lamps.

Early evening. Summer.

The room darkens during the course of the play.
The lamplight intensifies.

By the end of the play the room and the garden
beyond are only dimly defined.
The lamplight has become very bright but does not
illumine the room.

DEVLIN *standing with drink.* REBECCA *sitting.*

Silence.

REBECCA

Well . . . for example . . . he would stand over me and clench his fist. And then he'd put his other hand on my neck and grip it and bring my head towards him. His fist . . . grazed my mouth. And he'd say, 'Kiss my fist.'

DEVLIN

And did you?

REBECCA

Oh yes. I kissed his fist. The knuckles. And then he'd open his hand and give me the palm of his hand . . . to kiss . . . which I kissed.

Pause.

And then I would speak.

DEVLIN

What did you say? You said what? What did you say?

Pause.

REBECCA

I said, 'Put your hand round my throat.' I murmured it through his hand, as I was kissing it, but he heard my voice, he heard it through his hand, he felt my voice in his hand, he heard it there.

Silence.

DEVLIN

And did he? Did he put his hand round your throat?

REBECCA

Oh yes. He did. He did. And he held it there, very gently, very gently, so gently. He adored me, you see.

DEVLIN

He adored you?

Pause.

What do you mean, he adored you? What do you mean?

Pause.

Are you saying he put no pressure on your throat? Is that what you're saying?

REBECCA

No.

DEVLIN

What then? What are you saying?

REBECCA

He put a little . . . pressure . . . on my throat, yes.
So that my head started to go back, gently but truly.

DEVLIN

And your body? Where did your body go?

REBECCA

My body went back, slowly but truly.

DEVLIN

So your legs were opening?

REBECCA

Yes.

Pause.

DEVLIN

Your legs were opening?

REBECCA

Yes.

Silence.

DEVLIN

Do you feel you're being hypnotised?

REBECCA

When?

DEVLIN

Now.

REBECCA

No.

DEVLIN

Really?

REBECCA

No.

DEVLIN

Why not?

REBECCA

Who by?

DEVLIN

By me.

REBECCA

You?

DEVLIN

What do you think?

REBECCA

I think you're a fuckpig.

DEVLIN

Me a fuckpig? Me! You must be joking.

REBECCA *smiles*.

REBECCA

Me joking? You must be joking.

Pause.

DEVLIN

You understand why I'm asking you these questions.
Don't you? Put yourself in my place. I'm compelled to
ask you questions. There are so many things I don't
know. I know nothing . . . about any of this. Nothing.
I'm in the dark. I need light. Or do you think my
questions are illegitimate?

Pause.

REBECCA

What questions?

Pause.

DEVLIN

Look. It would mean a great deal to me if you could define him more clearly.

REBECCA

Define him? What do you mean, define him?

DEVLIN

Physically. I mean, what did he actually look like? If you see what I mean? Length, breadth . . . that sort of thing. Height, width. I mean, quite apart from his . . . disposition, whatever that may have been . . . or his character . . . or his spiritual . . . standing . . . I just want, well, I need . . . to have a clearer idea of him . . . well, not a clearer idea . . . just an idea, in fact . . . because I have absolutely no idea . . . as things stand . . . of what he looked like.
I mean, what did he *look like*? Can't you give him a shape for me, a concrete shape? I want a concrete image of him, you see . . . an image I can carry about with me. I mean, all you can talk of are his hands, one hand over your face, the other on the back of your neck, then the first one on your throat. There must be more to him than hands. What about eyes? Did he have any eyes?

REBECCA

'What colour?

Pause.

34

DEVLIN

That's precisely the question I'm asking you . . . my
darling.

REBECCA

How odd to be called darling. No one has ever called
me darling. Apart from my lover.

DEVLIN

I don't believe it.

REBECCA

You don't believe what?

DEVLIN

I don't believe he ever called you darling.

Pause.

Do you think my use of the word is illegitimate?

REBECCA

What word?

DEVLIN

Darling.

REBECCA

Oh yes, you called me darling. How funny.

35

DEVLIN

Funny? Why?

REBECCA

Well, how can you possibly call me darling? I'm not
your darling.

DEVLIN

Yes you are.

REBECCA

Well I don't want to be your darling. It's the last thing
I want to be. I'm nobody's darling.

DEVLIN

That's a song.

REBECCA

What?

DEVLIN

'I'm nobody's baby now'.

REBECCA

It's 'You're nobody's baby now'. But anyway, I didn't
use the word baby.

Pause.

I can't tell you what he looked like.

DEVLIN

Have you forgotten?

REBECCA

No. I haven't forgotten. But that's not the point.
Anyway, he went away years ago.

DEVLIN

Went away? Where did he go?

REBECCA

His job took him away. He had a job.

DEVLIN

What was it?

REBECCA

What?

DEVLIN

What kind of job was it? What job?

REBECCA

I think it had something to do with a travel agency.
I think he was some kind of courier. No. No, he
wasn't. That was only a part-time job. I mean that
was only part of the job in the agency. He was quite
high up, you see. He had a lot of responsibilities.

Pause.

DEVLIN

What sort of agency?

REBECCA

A travel agency.

DEVLIN

What sort of travel agency?

REBECCA

He was a guide, you see. A guide.

DEVLIN

A tourist guide?

Pause.

REBECCA

Did I ever tell you about that place . . . about the time he took me to that place?

DEVLIN

What place?

REBECCA

I'm sure I told you.

DEVLIN

No. You never told me.

REBECCA

How funny. I could swear I had. Told you.

DEVLIN

You haven't told me anything. You've never spoken about him before. You haven't told me anything.

Pause.

What place?

REBECCA

Oh, it was a kind of factory, I suppose.

DEVLIN

What do you mean, a kind of factory? Was it a factory or wasn't it? And if it was a factory, what kind of factory was it?

REBECCA

Well, they were making things – just like any other factory. But it wasn't the usual kind of factory.

DEVLIN

Why not?

REBECCA

They were all wearing caps . . . the workpeople . . . soft caps . . . and they took them off when he came in, leading me, when he led me down the alleys between the rows of workpeople.

DEVLIN

They took their caps off? You mean they doffed them?

REBECCA

Yes.

DEVLIN

Why did they do that?

REBECCA

He told me afterwards it was because they had such great respect for him.

DEVLIN

Why?

REBECCA

Because he ran a really tight ship, he said. They had total faith in him. They respected his . . . purity, his . . . conviction. They would follow him over a cliff and into the sea, if he asked them, he said. And sing in a chorus, as long as he led them. They were in fact very musical, he said.

DEVLIN

What did they make of you?

REBECCA

Me? Oh, they were sweet. I smiled at them. And immediately every single one of them smiled back.

Pause.

The only thing was – the place was so damp. It was exceedingly damp.

DEVLIN

And they weren't dressed for the weather?

REBECCA

No.

Pause.

DEVLIN

I thought you said he worked for a travel agency?

REBECCA

And there was one other thing. I wanted to go to the bathroom. But I simply couldn't find it. I looked everywhere. I'm sure they had one. But I never found out where it was.

Pause.

He did work for a travel agency. He was a guide. He used to go to the local railway station and walk down the platform and tear all the babies from the arms of their screaming mothers.

Pause.

DEVLIN

Did he?

Silence.

REBECCA

By the way, I'm terribly upset.

DEVLIN

Are you? Why?

REBECCA

Well, it's about that police siren we heard a couple of minutes ago.

DEVLIN

What police siren?

REBECCA

Didn't you hear it? You must have heard it. Just a couple of minutes ago.

DEVLIN

What about it?

REBECCA

Well, I'm just terribly upset.

Pause.

I'm just incredibly upset.

Pause.

Don't you want to know why? Well, I'm going to tell
you anyway. If I can't tell you who can I tell? Well,
I'll tell you anyway. It just hit me so hard. You see . . .
as the siren faded away in my ears I knew it was
becoming louder and louder for somebody else.

DEVLIN

You mean that it's always being heard by somebody,
somewhere? Is that what you're saying?

REBECCA

Yes. Always. For ever.

DEVLIN

Does that make you feel secure?

REBECCA

No! It makes me feel insecure! Terribly insecure.

DEVLIN

Why?

REBECCA

I hate it fading away. I hate it echoing away. I hate
it leaving me. I hate losing it. I hate somebody else
possessing it. I want it to be mine, all the time.
It's such a beautiful sound. Don't you think?

43

DEVLIN

Don't worry, there'll always be another one. There's one on its way to you now. Believe me. You'll hear it again soon. Any minute.

REBECCA

Will I?

DEVLIN

Sure. They're very busy people, the police. There's so much for them to do. They've got so much to take care of, to keep their eye on. They keep getting signals, mostly in code. There isn't one minute of the day when they're not charging around one corner or another in the world, in their police cars, ringing their sirens. So you can take comfort from that, at least. Can't you? You'll never be lonely again. You'll never be without a police siren. I promise you.

Pause.

Listen. This chap you were just talking about . . . I mean this chap you and I have been talking about . . . in a manner of speaking . . . when exactly did you meet him? I mean when did all this happen exactly? I haven't . . . how can I put this . . . quite got it into focus. Was it before you knew me or after you knew me? That's a question of some importance. I'm sure you'll appreciate that.

REBECCA

By the way, there's something I've been dying to tell
you.

DEVLIN

What?

REBECCA

It was when I was writing a note, a few notes for the
laundry. Well . . . to put it bluntly . . . a laundry list.
Well, I put my pen on that little coffee table and it
rolled off.

DEVLIN

No?

REBECCA

It rolled right off, onto the carpet. In front of my eyes.

DEVLIN

Good God.

REBECCA

This pen, this perfectly innocent pen.

DEVLIN

You can't know it was innocent.

REBECCA

Why not?

DEVLIN

Because you don't know where it had been. You don't know how many other hands have held it, how many other hands have written with it, what other people have been doing with it. You know nothing of its history. You know nothing of its parents' history.

REBECCA

A pen has no parents.

Pause.

DEVLIN

You can't sit there and say things like that.

REBECCA

I can sit here.

DEVLIN

You can't sit there and say things like that.

REBECCA

You don't believe I'm entitled to sit here? You don't think I'm entitled to sit in this chair, in the place where I live?

DEVLIN

I'm saying that you're not entitled to sit in that chair or in or on any other chair and say things like that and it doesn't matter whether you live here or not.

REBECCA

I'm not entitled to say things like what?

DEVLIN

That that pen was innocent.

REBECCA

You think it was guilty?

Silence.

DEVLIN

I'm letting you off the hook. Have you noticed?
I'm letting you slip. Or perhaps it's me who's slipping.
It's dangerous. Do you notice? I'm in a quicksand.

REBECCA

Like God.

DEVLIN

God? God? You think God is sinking into a quicksand?
That's what I would call a truly disgusting perception.
If it can be dignified by the word perception. Be careful
how you talk about God. He's the only God we have.
If you let him go he won't come back. He won't even
look back over his shoulder. And then what will you
do? You know what it'll be like, such a vacuum?
It'll be like England playing Brazil at Wembley and
not a soul in the stadium. Can you imagine? Playing
both halves to a totally empty house. The game of the
century. Absolute silence. Not a soul watching.

47

Absolute silence. Apart from the referee's whistle and a fair bit of fucking and blinding. If you turn away from God it means that the great and noble game of soccer will fall into permanent oblivion. No score for extra time after extra time after extra time, no score for time everlasting, for time without end. Absence. Stalemate. Paralysis. A world without a winner.

Pause.

I hope you get the picture.

Pause.

Now let me say this. A little while ago you made . . . shall we say . . . you made a somewhat oblique reference to your bloke . . . your lover? . . . and babies and mothers, et cetera. And platforms. I inferred from this that you were talking about some kind of atrocity. Now let me ask you this. What authority do you think you yourself possess which would give you the right to discuss such an atrocity?

REBECCA

I have no such authority. Nothing has ever happened to me. Nothing has ever happened to any of my friends. I have never suffered. Nor have my friends.

DEVLIN

Good.

Pause.

Shall we talk more intimately? Let's talk about more
intimate things, let's talk about something more
personal, about something within your own immediate
experience. I mean, for example, when the hairdresser
takes your head in his hands and starts to wash your
hair very gently and to massage your scalp, when he
does that, when your eyes are closed and he does that,
he has your entire trust, doesn't he? It's not just your
head which is in his hands, is it, it's your life, it's your
spiritual . . . welfare.

Pause.

So you see what I wanted to know was this . . . when
your lover had his hand on your throat, did he remind
you of your hairdresser?

Pause.

I'm talking about your lover. The man who tried to
murder you.

REBECCA

Murder me?

DEVLIN

Do you to death.

REBECCA

No, no. He didn't try to murder me. He didn't want to murder me.

DEVLIN

He suffocated you and strangled you. As near as makes no difference. According to your account. Didn't he?

REBECCA

No, no. He felt compassion for me. He adored me.

Pause.

DEVLIN

Did he have a name, this chap? Was he a foreigner? And where was I at the time? What do you want me to understand? Were you unfaithful to me? Why didn't you confide in me? Why didn't you confess? You would have felt so much better. Honestly. You could have treated me like a priest. You could have put me on my mettle. I've always wanted to be put on my mettle. It used to be one of my lifetime ambitions. Now I've missed my big chance. Unless all this happened before I met you. In which case you have no obligation to tell me anything. Your past is not my business. I wouldn't dream of telling you about my past. Not that I had one. When you lead a life of scholarship you can't be bothered with the humorous realities, you know, tits, that kind of thing. Your mind is on other things, have you got an attentive landlady, can she come up with bacon and eggs after eleven o'clock at night, is the bed warm, does the sun rise in the right direction, is the soup cold? Only once in a blue moon do you wobble the chambermaid's bottom, on the assumption there is one – chambermaid not bottom – but of course none of this applies when you have a wife. When you have a wife you let thought, ideas and reflection take their course. Which means you never let the best man win. Fuck the best man, that's always been my motto. It's the man who ducks his head and moves on through no matter what wind or weather who gets there in the end. A man with guts and application.

Pause.

A man who doesn't give a shit.
A man with a rigid sense of duty.

Pause.

There's no contradiction between those last two statements. Believe me.

Pause.

Do you follow the drift of my argument?

REBECCA

Oh yes, there's something I've forgotten to tell you. It was funny. I looked out of the garden window, out

of the window into the garden, in the middle of
summer, in that house in Dorset, do you remember?
Oh no, you weren't there. I don't think anyone else
was there. No. I was all by myself. I was alone. I was
looking out of the window and I saw a whole crowd
of people walking through the woods, on their way to
the sea, in the direction of the sea. They seemed to be
very cold, they were wearing coats, although it was
such a beautiful day. A beautiful, warm, Dorset day.
They were carrying bags. There were . . . guides . . .
ushering them, guiding them along. They walked
through the woods and I could see them in the distance
walking across the cliff and down to the sea. Then
I lost sight of them. I was really quite curious so I went
upstairs to the highest window in the house and
I looked way over the top of the treetops and I could
see down to the beach. The guides . . . were ushering
all these people across the beach. It was such a lovely
day. It was so still and the sun was shining. And I saw
all these people walk into the sea. The tide covered
them slowly. Their bags bobbed about in the waves.

DEVLIN

When was that? When did you live in Dorset? I've
never lived in Dorset.

Pause.

REBECCA

Oh by the way somebody told me the other day that
there's a condition known as mental elephantiasis.

52

DEVLIN

What do you mean, 'somebody told you'? What do you
mean, 'the other day'? What are you talking about?

REBECCA

This mental elephantiasis means that when you spill an
ounce of gravy, for example, it immediately expands
and becomes a vast sea of gravy. It becomes a sea
of gravy which surrounds you on all sides and you
suffocate in a voluminous sea of gravy. It's terrible.
But it's all your own fault. You brought it upon
yourself. You are not the *victim* of it, you are the *cause*
of it. Because it was you who spilt the gravy in the
first place, it was you who handed over the bundle.

Pause.

DEVLIN

The what

REBECCA

The bundle.

Pause.

DEVLIN

So what's the question? Are you prepared to drown
in your own gravy? Or are you prepared to die for
your country? Look. What do you say, sweetheart?
Why don't we go out and drive into town and take
in a movie?

REBECCA

That's funny, somewhere in a dream . . . a long time ago . . . I heard someone calling me sweetheart.

Pause.

I looked up. I'd been dreaming. I don't know whether I looked up in the dream or as I opened my eyes. But in this dream a voice was calling. That I'm certain of. This voice was calling me. It was calling me sweetheart.

Pause.

Yes.

Pause.

I walked out into the frozen city. Even the mud was frozen. And the snow was a funny colour. It wasn't white. Well, it was white but there were other colours in it. It was as if there were veins running through it. And it wasn't smooth, as snow is, as snow should be. It was bumpy. And when I got to the railway station I saw the train. Other people were there.

Pause.

And my best friend, the man I had given my heart to, the man I knew was the man for me the moment we met, my dear, my most precious companion,

I watched him walk down the platform and tear all the babies from the arms of their screaming mothers.

Silence.

DEVLIN
Did you see Kim and the kids?

She looks at him.

You were going to see Kim and the kids today.

She stares at him.

Your sister Kim and the kids.

REBECCA
Oh, Kim! And the kids, yes. Yes. Yes, of course I saw them. I had tea with them. Didn't I tell you?

DEVLIN
No.

REBECCA
Of course I saw them.

Pause.

DEVLIN
How were they?

55

REBECCA

Ben's talking.

DEVLIN

Really? What's he saying?

REBECCA

Oh, things like 'My name is Ben'. Things like that.
And 'Mummy's name is Mummy'. Things like that.

DEVLIN

What about Betsy?

REBECCA

She's crawling.

DEVLIN

No, really?

REBECCA

I think she'll be walking before we know where we
are. Honestly.

DEVLIN

Probably talking too. Saying things like 'My name is
Betsy'.

REBECCA

Yes, of course I saw them. I had tea with them. But
oh . . . my poor sister . . . she doesn't know what to do.

DEVLIN

What do you mean?

REBECCA

Well, he wants to come back . . . you know . . . he
keeps phoning and asking her to take him back.
He says he can't bear it, he says he's given the other
one up, he says he's living quite alone, he's given the
other one up.

DEVLIN

Has he?

REBECCA

He says he has. He says he misses the kids.

Pause.

DEVLIN

Does he miss his wife?

REBECCA

He says he's given the other one up. He says it was
never serious, you know, it was only sex.

DEVLIN

Ah.

Pause.

And Kim?

Pause.

And Kim?

REBECCA

She'll never have him back. Never. She says she'll
never share a bed with him again. Never. Ever.

DEVLIN

Why not?

REBECCA

Never ever.

DEVLIN

But why not?

REBECCA

Of course I saw Kim and the kids. I had tea with
them. Why did you ask? Did you think I didn't see
them?

DEVLIN

No. I didn't know. It's just that you said you were
going to have tea with them.

REBECCA

Well, I did have tea with them! Why shouldn't I? She's
my sister.

Pause.

58

Guess where I went after tea? To the cinema. I saw a film.

DEVLIN

Oh? What?

REBECCA

A comedy.

DEVLIN

Uh-huh? Was it funny? Did you laugh?

REBECCA

Other people laughed. Other members of the audience. It was funny.

DEVLIN

But you didn't laugh?

REBECCA

Other people did. It was a comedy. There was a girl . . . you know . . . and a man. They were having lunch in a smart New York restaurant. He made her smile.

DEVLIN

How?

REBECCA

Well . . . he told her jokes.

DEVLIN

Oh, I see.

REBECCA

And then in the next scene he took her on an expedition to the desert, in a caravan. She'd never lived in a desert before, you see. She had to learn how to do it.

Pause.

DEVLIN

Sounds very funny.

REBECCA

But there was a man sitting in front of me, to my right. He was absolutely still throughout the whole film. He never moved, he was rigid, like a body with rigor mortis, he never laughed once, he just sat like a corpse. I moved far away from him, I moved as far away from him as I possibly could.

Silence.

DEVLIN

Now look, let's start again. We live here. You don't live . . . in Dorset . . . or *anywhere else*. You live here with me. This is our house. You have a very nice sister. She lives close to you. She has two lovely kids. You're their aunt. You like that.

Pause.

You have a wonderful garden. You love your garden.
You created it all by yourself. You have truly green
fingers. You also have beautiful fingers.

Pause.

Did you hear what I said? I've just paid you a
compliment. In fact I've just paid you a number of
compliments. Let's start again.

REBECCA

I don't think we can start again. We started . . . a long
time ago. We started. We can't start *again*. We can end
again.

DEVLIN

But we've never ended.

REBECCA

Oh, we have. Again and again and again. And we can
end again. And again and again. And again.

DEVLIN

Aren't you misusing the word 'end'? End means end.
You can't end 'again'. You can only end once.

REBECCA

No. You can end once and then you can end again.

61

Silence.

(*singing softly*) 'Ashes to ashes' –

DEVLIN

'And dust to dust' –

REBECCA

'If the women don't get you' –

DEVLIN

'The liquor must.'

Pause.

I always knew you loved me.

REBECCA

Why?

DEVLIN

Because we like the same tunes.

Silence.

Listen.

Pause.

Why have you never told me about this lover of yours before this? I have the right to be very angry indeed.

Do you realise that? I have the right to be very angry indeed. Do you understand that?

Silence.

REBECCA

Oh by the way there's something I meant to tell you. I was standing in a room at the top of a very tall building in the middle of town. The sky was full of stars. I was about to close the curtains but I stayed at the window for a time looking up at the stars. Then I looked down. I saw an old man and a little boy walking down the street. They were both dragging suitcases. The little boy's suitcase was bigger than he was. It was a very bright night. Because of the stars. The old man and the little boy were walking down the street. They were holding each other's free hand. I wondered where they were going. Anyway, I was about to close the curtains but then I suddenly saw a woman following them, carrying a baby in her arms.

Pause.

Did I tell you the street was icy? It was icy. So she had to tread very carefully. Over the bumps. The stars were out. She followed the man and the boy until they turned the comer and were gone.

Pause.

She stood still. She kissed her baby. The baby was a girl.

Pause.

She kissed her.

Pause.

She listened to the baby's heartbeat. The baby's heart
was beating.

*The light in the room has darkened. The lamps are
very bright.*

REBECCA *sits very still.*

The baby was breathing.

Pause.

I held her to me. She was breathing. Her heart was
beating.

*Devlin goes to her. He stands over her and looks
down at her. He clenches his fist and holds it in front
of her face. He puts his left hand behind her neck and
grips it. He brings her head towards his fist. His fist
touches her mouth.*

DEVLIN

Kiss my fist.

She does not move.

He opens his hand and places the palm of his hand on her mouth.

She does not move.

DEVLIN

Speak. Say it. Say 'Put your hand round my throat.'

She does not speak.

Ask me to put my hand round your throat.

She does not speak or move.

He puts his hand on her throat. He presses gently. Her head goes back.

They are still.

She speaks. There is an echo. His grip loosens.

REBECCA

They took us to the trains

ECHO

the trains

He takes his hand from her throat.

REBECCA

They were taking the babies away

ECHO

the babies away

Pause.

REBECCA

I took my baby and wrapped it in my shawl

ECHO

my shawl

REBECCA

And I made it into a bundle

ECHO

a bundle

REBECCA

And I held it under my left arm

ECHO

my left arm

Pause.

REBECCA

And I went through with my baby

ECHO

my baby

Pause.

REBECCA

But the baby cried out

ECHO

cried out

REBECCA

And the man called me back

ECHO

called me back

REBECCA

And he said what do you have there

ECHO

have there

REBECCA

He stretched out his hand for the bundle

ECHO

for the bundle

REBECCA

And I gave him the bundle

ECHO

the bundle

REBECCA

And that's the last time I held the bundle

ECHO

the bundle

Silence.

REBECCA

And we got on the train

ECHO

the train

REBECCA

And we arrived at this place

ECHO

this place

REBECCA

And I met a woman I knew

ECHO

I knew

REBECCA

And she said what happened to your baby

ECHO

your baby

REBECCA

Where is your baby

ECHO

your baby

REBECCA

And I said what baby

ECHO

what baby

REBECCA

I don't have a baby

ECHO

a baby

REBECCA

I don't know of any baby

ECHO

of any baby

Pause.

REBECCA

I don't know of any baby

Long silence.

Blackout.